WAKE UP TO WORK

Geoff S.

SCRIPTURE UNION

Scripture Union, 207–209 Queensway, Bletchley, MK2 2EB, England.

© Geoff Shattock 1999

First published 1999

ISBN 1 85999 309 5

British Library Cataloguing-in-Publication Data
A catalogue record for this book is available from the British Library.

Cover design by David Lund.
Printed and bound in Great Britain by Cox & Wyman, Reading, Berkshire.

CONTENTS

FILE 4   Waking up to work

FILE 5   Closure

This book is dedicated with love and gratitude to my wife Maria – my best friend and co-worker.

Special thanks to:

The WorkNet Partnership board, for turning up, putting up and keeping up.

Simon and Jo Constantine, who put the fun back into work.

Roger Simpson, Phil Rowlands, Peter Anderson and Derek Cook for waking me up to evangelism.

Maureen Rose, for crossing the road and getting involved.

David Spriggs, for suggesting me in the first place.

David and Peggy Heron, for lending me a place by the sea to write.

All those who told their stories for the cases in point.

Anne Niblock and Maria Shattock, for typing the texts.

Jonathan Stunt and Godfrey Rust, for reading the texts.

Jo Campbell (Editor) and Andrew Clark (Managing Editor), for honing the product.

Colleagues down the years with whom I've shared the best and worst of times.

Extra special thanks to my daughter Suzy, who wakes me up to all kinds of things, especially when not at work.

KEY TO THE BOOK

FILES AND MEMOS

This book is arranged in five files, each one a collection of related subjects called 'memos'. There are thirty-one memos in all: if you are really busy, you can read one a day for a month (as long as it's not September, April, June, November or February). No memo is very long, so you can read each file a bit at a time.

INTERACTIVES

Dotted throughout the text you will find short exercises or sets of questions which you can use either on your own or in a small group. You don't have to follow all the instructions to the letter, but it's well worth giving them some attention.

CASES IN POINT

These are real-life, true stories from the workplace. In some, I've changed the names of the individuals involved. I've not put a lot of interpretation into the stories; I've just told them. I think they speak for themselves and you can take from them what you want. Although they come near relevant text, they illustrate several aspects of the theme of this book.

EXECUTIVE SUMMARIES FOR THE BUSY AND LAZY

These are exactly what they say they are. It's your money and your time; if it helps, read only these.

RESOURCES

A few suggestions to help you keep on waking up to work.

FOREWORD

This series, 'Relating Good News', is intended to help us maximise the opportunities for evangelism in our relationships and to become more relational people. Today, quality relationships have proved to be the most effective way of winning people to Christ. Jesus himself understood the value of good relationships for his ministry, as did Paul – someone who knew well how important it was to 'become all things to all people so that some may believe'. We too must recognise that, in an age when 'the medium is the message', the quality of our relationships will greatly affect our ability to communicate an adequate gospel.

Not all our friendships will be intense and long-lasting, yet we can learn how to make the most of the brief encounters, too. The books in this series, therefore, are about equipping us to be effective in sharing God's good news within the whole variety of relationships we may have. If you want to be better at relating, if you long to see your relationships honour Christ, if you desire to see the people you know become friends of Christ, my prayer is that here you will find much to help you as you seek to share your faith as well as your friendship.

David Spriggs

THE WORKING CHRISTIAN – IDEALLY PLACED FOR FAITH

If you would win a man to your cause you must first convince him that you are his sincere friend.

Abraham Lincoln

MEMO 1
Subject: Front line or bottom line

See if this description rings any bells with you.

The prayer meeting closes. You're usually too busy to make it, but this time you did. You've prayed for the minister, the Peruvian missionaries and the youth worker. You've prayed for the senior women's fellowship's total abstinence union day-trip to Nuneaton Priory. And tomorrow you wake up to work. God's interested in the youth worker and the women's fellowship but not, it seems, in your job. You even feel guilty sometimes about the money you make, which is certainly more than that earned by the minister, the Peruvian missionaries or the youth worker. Perhaps one day you will receive a call from God: in the meantime, your calls come via the switchboard.

Travelling in the next morning you reflect on how fulfilling it might be to serve the Lord working on the front line – but right now you have to serve the board working on the bottom line. Still, there are opportunities for witness – when the church has its mission-minded moments. You help in the worship service occasionally, and the house group has fellowship times in your home (which is more than you do, because it's hard to get there in time). They've just had a training day on evangelism and, when the evenings get lighter, you may get a chance to try it out on some unsuspecting local people on their doorsteps.

Everything you have been taught about your faith implies that it is a 24-hour, seven-day affair. You believe that your faith – like a lap-top or a mobile – is portable: it's not confined to church or home life, and should be expressed everywhere. But somehow it's not yet fully connected to your work. If you had more time to think about this, you could probably figure out where the blockages lie. You have a sneaking suspicion that there ought to be a better way of being a Christian at work; but for now you have to concentrate on just being at work. A day is coming, you promise yourself, when you'll find a sensible starting point and set about connecting your faith to your work in a way that really satisfies you.

That day has come. You can keep your promise. You've found this book. The starting point is friendship evangelism. As you'll see, this is an ideal place to begin connecting faith to work. It is my hope that, as you proceed through this uncomplicated book, you will discover profound truths that will become the tools you need to improve the connection. I'll start by telling you a little of my own story…

● ● ● ● ● ● ● ● ● ● ● ● ● ● ● ●

MEMO 2
Subject: Overcoming our own hypocrisies

I do not know his name, but there is a man in Surrey who accidentally helped me, under God, to set many Christians free in their thinking and practice of friendship evangelism in the workplace. The irony is that he felt himself to be a failure. When I met him, his whole manner was touched with despair and frustration. Little does he know it, but the conversation we had that summer evening changed my life permanently.

I was talking to a group of people gathered in a home. They were all from a church which will remain nameless, except that it was a big Baptist church in Guildford, down by the river! We were discussing witness in the workplace, when this man spoke up from the back of the lounge. 'If only I was living a more dynamic and powerful Christian life. My witness would be so much more effective,' he said.

Not too sure what to say to him, I replied with a question: 'What kind of Christian life *are* you living?'

'Well,' he said, 'sometimes I'm sure and sometimes I doubt. Sometimes I get it right and sometimes I get it wrong. Sometimes I'm really getting somewhere and then I blow it.'

'Well,' I said, 'why don't you tell them *that*?'

As the words came out of my mouth, I heard them for the first time. I'd never given this answer before, so it was as much news to me as it was to him. This was around eighteen years ago. That conversation has had such a profound effect on my life, I've not stopped working on its implications since. Whether my replies helped him or not, I do not know.

Witnessing, at its most basic, is communicating to people what it is really like to be a Christian. This is such a simple truth, yet most of us keep forgetting it. I suppose part of the explanation for this is that in a spiritual war zone such as witnessing, this kind of truth will be one of the first casualties.

The lie most of us have come to believe is that 'witnessing' means telling (or showing) people what we think it *ought* to be like to be a Christian. This lie has done so much damage and tied so many in knots that it needs to be exposed, hung, drawn and quartered, and, like Guy Fawkes, its memory shot up in flames every year.

Let's be honest. We all know how to fail in the Christian life: to make mistakes at work, to slip up or blow up inappropriately. Who among us can claim always to have done what is right, honest or appropriate? But failure must not paralyse us. If failure and weakness are going to paralyse us in owning up to our Christian faith, then not only have we missed the point of being a Christian (ie that we are rescued not by our cleverness or merits but by Christ) but we're not going to communicate the real picture to those around us.

We're all experts at missing opportunities. Which of us has not thought of the right words to say only on the way home after a conversation with a colleague? We all have reached at least A'level standard in guilt in relation to the Christian life and witness, and some of us are masters of it. We fear that another sermon or book full of exhortation to commitment will only add to our quota of guilt. We're tired of being told that we should be more effective in evangelism. We *know* that. What we want to know is *how*! What I'm suggesting is that a huge part of the 'how' is bound up with that conversation I had in Surrey, about honesty leading to a type of witness which includes our failures without being paralysed by them.

Whatever your level of expertise or guilt in relation to the workplace, I'm going to invite you, in these pages, to join me in building a bridge between your current competence and that liberating truth I discovered in Surrey. This is not as easy as it sounds, but it's nowhere near as difficult as you may have been led to believe. This particular bridge will require that we all do some building. When the bridge is completed, we'll stand together and look down from our new vantage point and see a raging river of doubts and fears, misunderstandings, regrets and rebellion flowing beneath us. I'll hope we'll wonder together why we ever thought the bridge over this river couldn't be built.

Before we start building I'd better lay some foundations. First, I am convinced that all witness and all evangelism is ultimately built on friendship. Gavin Reid, in his excellent book *Good News to Share*, identifies the influence of Christian parents and of Christian friends as the two most significant factors in bringing people to faith. In 1992 John Finney, in *Finding Faith Today*, discovered the same: family and friends are a key influence in people coming to faith. Even where some of those questioned cited a church minister as the key factor, you can be sure that this minister was a friend to those he or she reached.

However you look at it, evangelism is about people reaching people. For people to reach people there has to be an element of trust. And for trust to make some sense it has to include friendship, however casual. More of this in File 2.

A second related aspect is that the primary friendship in the witnessing or evangelism process may not always be yours. It has always encouraged me to realise that God has a bigger view of these things than I. Often when talking to someone about faith, they will speak of another person whom they respect or love, who is also a Christian. So, although your relationship with your colleague may be quite shallow, somewhere in their journey to faith there will be a friend or fellow traveller influencing them. Foundation is a good metaphor here, since this influence is often a hidden factor.

Third, however frustrating it may be, some people, maybe even the majority, will reject the core of what you stand for. This must not deter you from friendship. True friendship is not based on the other person coming round to your point of view but on trust, respect and, dare I say it, love. Although you may want your colleague to become a Christian, the level of friendship must not be determined by his or her degree of interest in your faith – that would not be befriending but selling.

The fourth foundation we must lay is the understanding that although there may be only one way to God through Jesus Christ, there are millions of ways to faith. Some people experience dramatic conversions; others gradual, almost imperceptible changes. Some take forever; others are born again on the spot. Some reject now and accept later; others never seem to respond. If you want some biblical analogies, some encounter Christ on the Damascus road (with a blinding flash), others on the Jericho road (as they lie battered and bruised), and still others on the Emmaus road (as the truth is explained to them). Most probably encounter Christ at a place where these roads meet. A Christian who is hung up on a formula will find life very exasperating and stressful. People are messy. They will neither be buttonholed nor pigeon-holed. They start in different places, take varying routes and – surprise, surprise – arrive at different times in all kinds of conditions.

Let's be clear. I'm not saying that all roads lead to God, nor that all religions and cults are valid. I am simply observing that people become Christians in different ways, and our relationship with them may only overlap with a small part of that process. And that's OK.

Before we race ahead, let me clarify the argument I am making. The Christian way is best communicated in the context of good quality relationships. This book is about the theory and practice of developing those relationships at work. This process is a part of the whole issue of integrating faith with work. To look at that whole issue will require several books: here you will find an excellent way in.

In addition, although the tone of this book is not meant to be guilt inducing or exhortationary, I am assuming that you realise the importance of the issue at hand. It really does matter that you communicate your faith, because people without Jesus Christ really are in trouble. This process of building good relationships at work is not some sort of optional extra for those who are that way inclined, although some people, because of their personalities, will find it much easier than others. This process has to be a way of life and of working.

If we're going to take any of this thinking to work with us, we'd better make sure we know something about the relationship-building process and see its connection to the biblical teaching on discipleship.

• CASE IN POINT •

Colin works in the public sector. A mature man with many years experience, he was asked by one of his seniors to convey a message to a colleague. The content of the message required that this colleague take a certain course of action. The message was conveyed and the action taken.

On reporting back to his senior, Colin received a surprise. 'Actually, Colin, the message wasn't true,' he was told, 'but I knew that if you conveyed it, it would be believed.' You don't need to be a genius to guess at Colin's reply. It hasn't happened again.

● ● ● ● ● ● ● ● ● ● ● ● ● ●

MEMO 3
Subject: Mission statements

At the end of the first recorded full week of work, God gave the founding partners of the human race an instruction: 'Go and multiply'. We've obeyed this instruction with great enthusiasm, and I'm sure we're reaching our targets because there are billions of us. Jump to the start of the New Testament and you'll find that, at the end of several years work on earth, Jesus said to his team, 'Go and make disciples.' We've still got some work to do on this one.

Both these instructions are based on similar principles. God says, 'I've made you into people – go and make some more'; Jesus says, 'I've made you into disciples – go and make some more'. God, it seems, wants us to carry on his work by multiplying what he has started. What's more, he has built into us the ability to do this. So, when you go to work you take with you the ability to reproduce what God has produced in you. 'Go and make some more,' he says. 'Go and make some duplicates or copies of who you are.'

Jesus gave two footnotes to his instructions at the end of Matthew's Gospel. First, all authority everywhere belongs to him. So you don't need anyone else's say-so to do this work. He says so. Second, he is coming with you – even to work: 'I will be with you always – everywhere'. Jesus is at your desk, cab, lab, classroom, courtroom, ward, workshop, assembly line, dealing room or dark room. He wants to work with you on this task of making some more of you.

By now several of you may have your hands raised in horror at the thought of making some more people like you (and without your boss's permission). Let me remind you that this is quite biblical.

INTERACTIVE 1

Have a look at these verses:

> 'I urge you to imitate me.' *(1 Corinthians 4:16)*

> 'Follow my example, as I follow the example of Christ.' *(1 Corinthians 11:1)*

'Join with others in following my example, brothers, and take note of those who live according to the pattern we gave you.' *(Philippians 3:17)*

'Whatever you have learned or received or heard from me, or seen in me – put it into practice.' *(Philippians 4:9)*

'You became imitators of us and of the Lord...' *(1 Thessalonians 1:6)*

Now ask yourself a few questions:

How do I feel about people imitating me?

What would it be like if my colleagues followed my example?

Am I confident that staff members/colleagues can see in me things they should put into practice?

In Athens, we're told in Acts, people became followers of Paul. Have you noticed, in your church family, how new Christians soon display a family likeness, picking up the characteristics of the Christians around them. That's how it works.

Now all these mission statements are saying the same thing: Christianity is reproduced by copying, following, modelling, showing. Don't misunderstand this. It is the Spirit of God who reproduces new life, but he has chosen to work through you, even at work.

Let's push this a bit further. The meaning here is not just 'Follow me' but 'Follow me as I follow Christ'. It's 'Copy me copying him', 'Model me modelling him'. Staying on-line with him will help you download data to others. Your effectiveness in this process will be greatly enhanced as you keep growing in your own discipleship. And, most importantly, this truth frees you to be yourself. It frees you to give to others what Christ has given to you.

'I'm no Paul,' I hear you say. No, and you're not supposed to be. You're you. You're the person God made, and you're the person Jesus is making. And that's OK. This modelling activity has to have a context because it cannot take place in a vacuum. Again, I would suggest to you that the best context is friendship.

Now would be a good time to consider what exactly we are supposed to be modelling or showing.

• **CASE IN POINT** •

Jenny was quite popular with her colleagues. Unfortunately, she was not too pleased with herself. She was experiencing some sexual difficulties, along with other personal problems, which were not helping her Christian growth. Internally, she felt at war with herself and fairly isolated from her fellow Christians.

Over lunch in the canteen her colleague, Sarah, turned to her out of the blue and said, 'It's good to have you around, Jenny. We always say when you arrive, "Here comes Jenny – here comes peace." '

MEMO 4
Subject: On being a Christian, full stop

Have you noticed that when a small group of Christians gather to pray for one another, they are often brutally honest? Requests are made for prayer concerning illness, family struggles or work issues. Fears of redundancy or adolescent rebellion are aired and sympathetic nods precede pastoral prayer. Now make that group evangelistic, add some non-Christians and listen to the conversation. 'Since I became a Christian I've found new joy and certainty – a meaning in life which stays with me.' 'I've discovered who I am and I never want to go back.' Is this the same group of people? It is, of course and both scenes are fact not fiction. But each plays out only half of the truth.

If you or I want to develop a healthy and honest approach to friendship evangelism in the workplace (or anywhere else for that matter), we have to ask and answer a very basic question, 'What is it really like to be a Christian?'

INTERACTIVE 2

Draw a line down the middle of a page. On one side, list the benefits and, on the other side, the costs of being a Christian. Add any aspects you like to build up a true picture of being a Christian. If you are a Christian or in a Christian group you're also asking the question, 'What is it like to be me or us?' Be brutally honest. Keep adding things until you or the group is satisfied. Now look at your list. It should contain the basic information you will need to communicate if you want others to know about being a Christian. You might like to discuss or think about how you feel about communicating that information.

● ● ● ● ● ● ● ● ● ● ● ● ●

Armed with our picture of the real Christian, let me tell you about some of my own less-than-real behaviour.

MEMO 5
Subject: Dealing with the stress of trying to be what we are not

Some time ago I was working with a Jewish man who happened to be physically very large and had a presence to match. For over eighteen months I had been 'witnessing' to him in overt verbal ways and, while we remained friends, he remained unmoved. He saw me one lunchtime in the dining room and commented that I looked depressed. Now at this particular point in my life I never admitted to anyone if I was struggling in any way. So it came as a great shock to me when I said, 'I am.' He stood back in horror. 'I thought Christians weren't supposed to get depressed,' he said.

'So did I,' I said. And there it was. I couldn't take it back. I felt my carefully worked-up images tumbling around me and my months of crafted conversations evaporating in the heat of the moment.

His reaction was startling. He offered to buy me a drink, and we adjourned to a bar for the best conversation he and I had ever experienced. There were many reasons for this, but in his mind there was a thought process developing. It went like this: 'He's a mess and he's a Christian – I'm a mess, maybe I could be a Christian.'

If you engaged with Interactive 2, you most likely came up with a picture of Christianity which included pleasure and pain. There is certainty and doubt, friendship and loneliness, success and disappointment in the Christian journey. There are times when you can pray and feel that God is in the room with you; at other times it feels like you're talking to the ceiling. Sometimes you sense a divine order about your life; at other times you feel a sense of quiet desperation and have no idea of what is going on. Facing up to the reality of the Christian life is not an optional extra, but an essential prerequisite to effective relationship building. You see, you can actually tell people what it is really like to be a Christian.

The fact that I could be honest with my colleague and still have a powerful witness was an immense relief to me. I even found that during the conversation he was a great help to me. It was a full four years later that I met the man in Surrey and finally started to realise what I was learning. At last I was able to build a bridge between my competence and the liberating truths of friendship evangelism.

If you've followed the plan so far, you should already have your foundations in place. Let's go to work on the rest.

• CASE IN POINT •

Laura is a psychotherapist with the NHS. Not surprisingly, most of the people referred to her are in serious difficulty and Jane was no exception when her GP referred her to the team. With a history of drug addiction, promiscuity and an abortion that had left her feeling she was a murderer, Jane, from a Sikh background, was moved to the top of the waiting list.

Laura recognised that Jane needed someone first to listen to her distress and, in contrast to her mother's response to the situation, to encourage her rather than label her as evil. After some months of therapy, Jane announced to Laura that she had become a Christian. Her new-found faith was enabling her to give up drugs, promiscuity and a boyfriend who wasn't really helping her. Jane recounted how she was now witnessing to others. She was clearly in love with God.

Several problems, however, persisted. Jane still hated her mother. She also still saw God as a harsh character and struggled with the feeling that she needed to prove herself to him. Even though she was a gifted person, Jane could not see those gifts for what they were – gifts from God.

Laura decided to work with Jane on several fronts, starting with forgiveness. She began gently encouraging her to see her mother in a new light. In addition, she sought to help Jane to see her gifts as coming from God and to learn to use them out of love for him rather than as a way of earning his approval. Laura is working to unravel confusion with professional integrity and to take Jane to a better place, which is exactly what she needs at the moment. At this point Laura has not specifically told Jane that she is a Christian. This does not mean, of course, that Jane doesn't know.

Executive summary for the busy or lazy

Many are uneasy about the split between faith and work; friendship is a good starting point to help us deal with this issue; friendship is the best starting point to communicate faith in the workplace; communicating faith through friendship requires total honesty; honesty requires communicating success and failure; honesty requires modelling our faith through our personalities; modelling our faith in this way requires that we know what it is really like to be a Christian; all this can be taken into the workplace.

THE BUSINESS OF FRIENDSHIP AND THE FRIENDSHIP OF BUSINESS

The greatest motivational act one person can do for another is to listen.

Roy Moody

MEMO 6
Subject: The friendship principle

It is vital that you be convinced of two things before we go any further: first, that friendship and trust are indispensable to the process of evangelism; second, that friendship is not incompatible with the workplace. If you have come to believe that evangelism can be 'done' to strangers by hit squads, or that professional and working relationships preclude friendship, I want to invite you to reconsider.

If you are going to make a purchase, a personal recommendation from a friend is highly influential. If you want some help in making a choice, you want someone to act like a friend to help you. In other words, friendship influences your choices. It's worth noting that the converse is true. An unfriendly or impersonal manner will turn you off a choice or a product.

If you've had your eyes open at work, you will have seen that the managers who get the most co-operation are friendly. The sales people who are most effective are friendly. The company that generates loyalty is the one that cares about people. It's the same when communicating the Christian message, and it's effective.

INTERACTIVE 3

Who convinces you to spend your money?

Take a moment to think about a purchase you have made or might make. For example, you might consider a holiday, a car or a washing machine. How would you go about choosing that particular item? What factors would influence your choice? Jot them down on a piece of paper or, if you are in a group, on an OHP/flip chart. Keep going until you have a reasonable list.

Now keep that list to hand and change the scene. You're in a shop and you want to buy something. What kind of person do you want the sales assistant to be? Again, think of a list of characteristics.

Now put both lists together and analyse your findings. The chances are that in the list from the first exercise you will have included factual-type influences such as *Which?* reports, technical information and prices. There will also be some issues of taste concerning the things you like about the item. In many of the groups I have worked with, personal recommendation has also played a key role. For an intangible purchase such as a holiday, a friend's recommendation becomes even more important. However many factors you listed, the chances are that a strong recommendation from a personal friend who already has the item or has been on the holiday will be highly influential.

If you look at your list from the second exercise, you have a profile of a particular type of person. Probably you have included things such as 'not pushy', 'courteous', 'knowledgeable', 'friendly', 'has my best interests in mind', and so on. Now roll all these characteristics up and ask what kind of people act like that in your life in general. The answer, of course, is friends.

● ● ● ● ● ● ● ● ● ● ● ● ● ●

MEMO 7
Subject: Power to all our friends

We've already referred to the work of Gavin Reid and John Finney in detailing the power of friendship. Let me add two further examples. An American survey, carried out as far back as 1982, revealed that people are influenced more by their friends than by the formal media. Interestingly, it also revealed the power of conversation (more on this in File 4). Much more recently a comprehensive survey by ICM, looking at stress in the workplace, reinforced this principle. Questioning 2,000 people in six industries, the researchers discovered that, in the middle of a whole range of stressors, one factor more than any other compensated pressurised employees. This factor was the friendship of a colleague. Friendship is not only possible in the workplace: if this survey is to be believed, it is indispensable.

Turning to the New Testament, we see this principle running throughout. The plan of rescue for us was not delivered by fax, letter or e-mail. It did not come in the form of a committee minute or even a booklet from heaven. Jesus Christ came *personally* to announce, be and implement the good news of freedom and encouragement. His enemies regularly accused him of being a friend of sinners, and so he was. Not long before he died he turned to his followers and said, 'I no longer call you servants but friends.' He knew that personal friendship based on trust is the way life works, and his life's work was dedicated to making friendship, both human and divine, a reality.

• CASE IN POINT •

John is a neonatal paediatrician in a teaching hospital. His job sometimes includes a roller-coaster ride of emotion, from seeing parent's extreme joy at the safe delivery of a baby to the the unspeakable pain associated with the loss of a child. Highly-skilled professional that he is, he will still sit and cry with distraught parents over the loss of a little life.

MEMO 8
Subject: High risks, high rewards

If you take this thinking about friendship seriously, you will find yourself embarking on an adventure. Running a variety of risks, you will discover that sometimes criticism will come your way for being present at workplace functions and absent from church. Your faith may be questioned as well as tested. You may fail and be judged for your faults or open yourself to all kinds of hurt and rejection.

But there are rewards. You will discover the world of people – their ambitions, motivations, joys and regrets. You will eventually earn respect and trust. You will find your faith confirmed and your spirit exhilarated with a sense of satisfaction because you are there, where the action really is, with the friend of sinners at your side. So let's keep building – if you dare.

Executive summary for the busy and lazy

Friendship and work can go together; friendly people influence others; friendship is a high risk, high reward activity.

THE WORKPLACE – IDEAL CONDITIONS FOR FAITH

There are two things people want more
than sex and money –
that's praise and recognition.

Mary Kay Ash

MEMO 9
Subject: Concerning time

Perform this simple calculation. Multiply your working hours by your working weeks by your working years, and you will have an idea of how much of your life you spend at work. You may like to add travel time, overtime and unsociable hours. The answer will vary greatly, but it could be as much as 100,000 hours. Whatever your figure, it's a fair chunk of your time on earth.

Time is also the currency of trust. Here's a great God-given opportunity: the very fact that you spend a significant amount of time at work provides you with the possibility of building meaningful relationships with your colleagues.

This is no hit-and-run environment. You have the time to be yourself and let your colleagues see you as you really are. Compare this with the amount of time you spend with your neighbours or even church friends, and you can see that it makes sense to consider the workplace as an environment for good quality relationships.

● ● ● ● ● ● ● ● ● ● ● ● ● ● ●

MEMO 10
Subject: Concerning community

Where do your colleagues find friendship? To a certain extent, the answer to this question will depend on their age. Certainly younger people, especially if they have moved home to take the job, will often seek companionship in the workplace. Increasingly, groups of people from the same place of work will socialise together or even go on holiday together. Many's the couple who, on their wedding day, reflect on the fact that they met at work. Of course, family ties may loosen the links to work relationships, but not always.

On another level, working practices, as we enter a new millenium, encourage informality and community. Flatter structures mean that old hierarchies are often (not always) removed, providing further opportunities for relationships that work. Gone are the days of the doffed hat and servile deference. Today is the era of team, learning organisations and partners. Employers know that pooled thinking and co-operation achieves better results all round. People-centred strategies are the order of the day (at least in theory). In short, the working environment is supposed to be more friendly.

● ● ● ● ● ● ● ● ● ● ● ● ● ● ●

MEMO 11
Subject: Work culture and world culture

If today's workplace culture lends itself to the development of working relationships and friendships, and friendship is a doorway to evangelism, it's worth developing two points here, to stimulate your thought.

First, consider the language that is now used by today's decision-makers. Here are some examples.

Mission statement
Companies are encouraging all of their staff to have a sense of purpose, to know why the company exists and what it stands for.

Values
Twenty years ago very few people, if any, spoke of having a set of values that governed the ethics and practice of a company or organisation. Today people are employed in some situations with the sole responsibility of developing and communicating values.

Investors in people
Schools, companies, health trusts and charities strive to achieve certain standards so that they can advertise the fact that people really matter to them and that they have developed working practices which are people-shaped.

Spirituality
Less defined but frequently cited, all kinds of consultants now talk of 'spirituality in the workplace'.

All these concepts are Christian. We too are on a *mission* or, more literally, a *commission* from Jesus Christ. He wants us to teach others to obey all he has commanded us (his *values*). He is the ultimate *investor in people*. He calls us to be like him, bringing our *spirituality* with us. These concepts, then, are part of our work culture and provide an environment in which we can express Christian values. Here is a superb opportunity for Christians to open up.

Second, our world culture (at least in the West) is today described as 'post-modern'. While this book is not the place to look at post-modernism in any detail, it is vital to note that one of the results of post-modern thinking is tolerance of a variety of viewpoints. Christians no longer have to shout to be heard but merely learn to add a clear message into the mix today and allow its quality to do the work. This may be frustrating for those of a dogmatic nature, but it does mean that we have a chance to advocate our faith as a practical, viable lifestyle without being sent to Coventry or thrown to the lions.

● ● ● ● ● ● ● ● ● ● ● ● ● ●

MEMO 12
Subject: Pressure, stress and struggling

Stress costs every employer around £550 per employee per year (according to a CBI survey in 1997). Huge numbers of employees are off sick on any one working day of the year. Downsizing has created the bizarre situation where those without a job have time on their hands, while those in work are facing ever increasing workloads. Performance-related measures mean that working practices are constantly monitored, from OFSTED inspections to personal reviews, with all the target-related burdens of market forces in between. Sunday night is a night of dread for many as they contemplate a week of unrelenting pressure on too low a salary, with little sense of meaning and value. Only a privileged few seem to speak of genuine job satisfaction. The bottom line has indeed become a tyrant.

There are two by-products of this situation. First, as a Christian, it provides you with a chance to prove in practice what you believe in theory, namely that God is your provider, even in the face of difficulties like downsizing and redundancy. Because you are not immune to any of these pressures, you are there in the boat with everyone else; but you also know who's in charge of the storm. This is not pious nonsense but rugged fact, and it will test even those of the strongest faith. Others are watching and we need to remember this.

Second, in these pressurised times people are often more willing to open up to a trustworthy Christian about their struggles. It is indeed a chance for you to be good news in the face of difficulty; in other words, to be a friend to others at work.

So rather than see only the ash in the furnace that is today's workplace, you can catch a glimpse of the golden opportunities God is entrusting to you.

These first three files have been about building a bridge for yourself. I hope that by now you will feel more confident as you look down from this vantage point. You may like to look back at the executive summaries, to refresh your memory.

The next files will also include some building work, but we're going to change the picture from that of a bridge to something else. We're going to shift the focus more towards building something others can use in this process of bringing friendship and evangelism to work.

• CASE IN POINT •

Michael was always there at work 'dos', whether they were after-hours parties or lunchtime gatherings. He genuinely enjoyed being with his non-Christian friends at work. On one such occasion, Dennis, who was a sort of social leader of the pack, spoke to Michael – in the gent's loo of all places. 'How come we never see you drunk? You enjoy a drink like the rest of us, don't you, Mike?'

'I'm happy when I'm sober,' was Mike's reply.

It was one of countless short conversations Mike and Dennis had in their three-year working relationship.

Mike was also very active in the Christian Union, putting on relevant presentations, so his witness was a mixture of personal and public. He moved on and eventually went into full-time ministry. A full twenty-one years later, he received a phone call from Dennis. 'I thought you might like to know, I've become a Christian,' said the voice on the phone. 'I know you were praying hard for us when we worked together.'

Executive summary for the busy and lazy

Time spent at work presents us with opportunities to develop friendship; workplace language lends itself to Christian communication; workplace pressures, while a challenge to faith, are also an opportunity for friendship.

WAKING UP TO WORK

If you are called to be a street sweeper, sweep streets as Michaelangelo painted or Beethoven composed music or Shakespeare wrote poetry. Sweep streets so well that all the hosts of heaven and earth will pause to say, 'Here lived a great sweeper who did his job well.'

Martin Luther King, Jr.

MEMO 13
Subject: Understanding your job description

John the Baptist was very good at his job. He saw himself as a road-builder. He got his job description from the book of Isaiah, and it included straightening out bends, filling in valleys, cutting through mountains and smoothing out the rough patches. (You can find his job description in Luke chapter 3.) Through his work he wanted to construct excellent highways for the Lord and he invited others to join him in this road-building programme.

His invitation still stands and provides us with a superb framework for understanding the nature of our own job descriptions. Assuming that you are now convinced of the need for good relationships as a context for natural Christian communication, how exactly are you supposed to put this into practice at work? The answer is be a road-builder.

We referred to the three roads to faith – the Damascus road, the Jericho road and the Emmaus road – in File 1, Memo 2. Now I'm going to spell this out in detail. The purpose of building these roads is to provide routes along which people can travel and meet the Lord. Whether or not they become Christians will depend on the nature of that meeting, but our job is to make sure that the roads are passable. For the sake of describing them, we'll need to look at each road separately. You will quickly realise, however, that these three roads intersect at many crossroads and roundabouts, and it's at these meeting points where much of the action occurs.

• CASE IN POINT •

Simon was recently interviewed for a job in an environmental company. He recognised that the interview was a good time to at least introduce the kind of approach he would take to the job. It was almost as a light-hearted comment that he quoted from the psalms: 'The earth is the Lord's and everything in it.' He got the job and is now in a position to bring Christian values into many lives by building up people's trust in him as he slowly follows through on his interview declarations. It's too early to say how everyone is reacting, but it's not too early to observe that he did the right thing.

MEMO 14
Subject: The Damascus commuter route –
faith that works in practice

The first of our highways is the Damascus road. You'll find it described in Acts chapter 9. Saul was on a business trip. Armed with the paperwork to close a take-over deal on the lives of many Damascene residents, he was a man with a purpose and he knew what to do. It was on this road, however, that he encountered the risen Lord. His life was totally transformed and, from then on, the Lord was going to tell him what to do. The delegation travelling with him saw something happen to him and were left quite literally speechless by the experience.

The Damascus road is all about changed lives. Saul became Paul and, from here on in, his working practices would be completely different. The Damascus experience included a supernatural encounter with Christ which worked itself into every department of his life. Its message is that Christianity works.

Here is a great truth. For your colleagues to encounter real Christianity, you will need to straighten, flatten, level and smooth a road which enables them to see that this Christianity, your Christianity, really works.

● ● ● ● ● ● ● ● ● ● ● ● ● ● ●

MEMO 15
Subject: Changed working practices

The Standard Occupation Classification System lists 3,800 job categories. Each one of them will have a catalogue of working practices. I can't possibly compile a list of Christian approaches to these millions of issues, but here are some pointers which may help you when you think about embarking on the Damascus project in your relationships at work.

First, learn to handle time well. Work involves selling your time to your employer. Christian working practices will attempt to give good value for money. This will include not doing too little work, but also not doing too much. It is no witness to work all hours and let everyone else around you pay for your workaholism. Jesus knew when to stop as well as when to go the extra mile. Remember that part of your witness will include how you balance your working and non-working life. Important though work may be, it is not your god. Others need to know that.

In a recent conversation with a trades union representative, I was challenged by him on the point that in the culture of 'presenteeism', some employers may actually penalise employees who appear to be going home 'too early'. In this same discussion, a Christian business owner confessed that he also valued employees by how much time they were prepared to put in. I suggested to them, as I suggest to you, that a Christian strategy in this context might include the Lord's enabling you, as an individual worker, to get an excellent day's work done in a reasonable amount of time. This is not a question of shirking responsibility but allowing the Lord to prosper your work. It's worth noting here, as in so many other situations, your grappling with the issue in an honest and open way is itself a witness to your colleagues.

Second, learn to handle money well. Christianity is not anti-money. It is true Jesus said that we cannot worship God and money, and Paul identified the love of money as the root of all kinds of evil. But nowhere is money itself seen as evil. The challenge for us as Christians is to learn to handle money in a godly manner. This could range from accurate claiming of expenses to paying creditors on time. For some, it may mean speaking up for ethical financial policies. If your job involves negotiation, then agreeing a fair price for a product or service – which leaves room for someone to

make a reasonable living – is all part of your working practices. One of the phrases that has saddened me most over the
last few years is 'I won't do business with Christians'. Often
this is said in the context of a financial transaction where
what might have been a superb opportunity to behave in a
Christian manner has been lost by elevating the pound to
divine status.

Third, learn to use words well. Telling the truth is not
always easy and, in some instances, very costly. John the
Baptist lost his life for telling the truth. In our places of work
the price may vary, but it's very refreshing to meet people
who keep their word when they promise to deliver. It's
encouraging to others when they see in you the humility to
apologise when you've made a mistake and to take responsibility for your actions. In some working cultures there is a
climate of honesty, in others there is not. But, irrespective of
the working culture, it's good to learn to tell the truth in a
complex world.

Fourth, learn to handle trouble well. Jesus promised us
that in this world we would have troubles: each day, he said,
had enough trouble of its own. How you as a Christian handle trouble will play a significant part in building the
Damascus road – for example, whether you lose your tem-
per or show assertive restraint, whether you confront or
avoid an important error in yourself or others. Your ability
to work hard to cover another's back, or to demonstrate your
trust in God when things look hopeless, are vital strategies
in your work as road-builder.

Don't forget that your Christianity also involves the
supernatural. Like the caterer at Cana, you may discover
that Jesus' presence in the workplace can result in problem-
solving beyond your abilities and skills. Praying when you
or someone else is in trouble will communicate your faith in
the Lord of the Damascus road, who can intervene where no
one else can.

Fifth, learn to enjoy your work. 'I saw', said Solomon,

'that there is nothing better for a man than to enjoy his work' (Eccl 3:22). No one in their right mind enjoys every single task at work, but I do believe that the Lord wants us to have a fundamental enjoyment of work (and life). In addition, because we are salt, light, yeast and good news (all of these things have a positive impact on their surroundings), we should be able to help others enjoy their work too.

It is worth noting that although Saul became Paul, he didn't lose his personality. He was still a driven, sometimes depressed, sometimes confrontational person. The Damascus project for you at work will involve demonstrating Christian working practices while still being yourself.

• CASE IN POINT •

Fiona was eighteen when she went to work as a secretary in a market research company. At that time she had had little meaningful contact with Christianity, and none that had made any impression on her. The working culture at the company included numerous office affairs, and conversations regularly included insults directed at absent wives or husbands.

Fiona's boss, Graham, was a Christian. She described him as the first intelligent Christian she had ever met. He exhibited a first-hand, thought-through version of Christianity which was new to her. As she recounted her experience of this job, she described three aspects of her relationship with her boss which had a profound influence on her life. The first was Graham's attitude to his wife, Tammy. He never ran her down in conversation as the other men did about their wives. Rather, he would talk about her with respect and love, freely admitting when he needed to consult with her about various matters. In a culture of affairs and insults, and coming from a background where infidelity was not uncommon, this example of a boss who loved his wife impressed Fiona deeply.

The second incident revealed Graham's hard edge. Fiona had been promised a pay rise by the board – a pay rise which had not materialised. And so, for this and other reasons, she sought alternative higher paid employment. On confiding to Graham that she now had a better offer, he promised to get her that pay rise if she agreed to stay. She agreed and Graham took the matter himself to the board. They refused. Graham was so adamant that promises should be honoured, he threatened to pull out of one of his own posts if this was not done. The board, seeing that he was serious, backed down. Fiona saw, first-hand, a man prepared to keep his word even at personal cost.

The third incident was very small. Some time during her employment Graham gave her a Bible. In it he wrote, 'One day you will need this.'

It was a full four years after leaving the company that Fiona became a Christian through many other influences. She and Graham remain friends.

● ● ● ● ● ● ● ● ● ● ● ● ● ●

MEMO 16
Subject: The Emmaus commuter route – demonstrating that it's true

We do not know exactly why the discouraged couple were making the trip on the Emmaus road (Luke 24:13 – 35), but we do know that it was on the first day of the working week.

As they were talking, Jesus came and joined in their discussion. It was as they walked and talked that he explained to them the reasons why they should have faith in the Christ. Such was his ability to explain the truth to them, their minds were fired and their hope restored.

The Emmaus road is all about explaining the truth. People in your workplace need to realise that Christianity is true.

Over the last twenty years I've spoken to thousands of people about communicating their faith. For most of them, this area of truth seems to hold the most fear. Peter urges us to be able to give reasons for the hope that is within us (1 Peter 3:15), yet many of us are afraid of not being able to answer the questions people ask. We feel that we will make fools of ourselves or say something incorrect. On top of this, we feel that it could spoil a working relationship or maybe alienate a colleague. In fact many of us are so afraid of verbal witness, we have amassed a number of reasons why we should *not* explain at work the hope within us. At this point it's worth noting that the Emmaus road experience was two trips in one. On the outward journey Jesus convinced the doubting disciples so that they had the courage to believe and to communicate their beliefs. So if you are a doubting disciple, let's remove a few of the boulders that may be blocking the way for you on the outward journey.

● ● ● ● ● ● ● ● ● ● ● ● ● ● ●

MEMO 17
Subject: 'My work is my witness'

This statement is one expression of a whole family of issues. It covers such things as 'They know where I stand', or 'I don't want to impose my views on others'. Of course, all these statements are true but they are not the whole truth.

People cannot guess what it means to be a Christian; you and I have to explain it. When people try to guess, they will come up with their own understandings, most of which will sound like 'Do as you would be done by' or 'I'm as good as the next person'. At Pentecost the corporate guess was that the disciples were drunk. Peter had to give reasons and explanations for what was going on, as do you at work.

• CASE IN POINT •

Ray was an atheist when he joined the company. Conversations with his Christian colleagues usually centred around Ray's view that God couldn't possibly be a father in the light of his own experience of a hypercritical, perfectionist father for whom even Ray's outstanding achievements were never good enough.

As they got to know him, his colleagues realised that they should pray for God to show himself to Ray in specific ways. A small prayer meeting already existed in the company to pray for company issues: prayers were very much centred around business strategies, finances and the realities of the business world. Ray asked if he could sit in as an observer.

While on a business trip to Spain, Ray met another couple of Christians, and together they had to take a long drive from Valencia to Madrid. Because the day was extremely hot and the car had no air conditioning, one of the Christians prayed before the journey that God would keep them cool – a prayer which was highly amusing to Ray.

On his return to the UK, Ray came back to the prayer meeting and recounted the story. The journey had been a complete puzzle to him. When he had looked out of the left or right side of the car, it was very sunny; but a cloud had hung over the car for the entire journey, and the travellers had subsequently stayed cool.

Ray has since become a Christian, after praying with one of those colleagues.

● ● ● ● ● ● ● ● ● ● ● ● ● ●

MEMO 18
Subject : 'I'm not here to evangelise'

This statement is perhaps the other side of the coin from Memo 17, and it is partly true. Everything you and I do speaks of who we are and what we believe. Any Christian who claims that he or she can be anywhere and not be communicating the Christian faith has missed the point. We are all witnessing all the time, and only sometimes will it be directly through what we say about our beliefs. The liberating aspect of this is that, in the context of natural, open and honest working relationships, we don't have to express all our beliefs in every conversation.

Hard on the heels of this statement is one such as 'My boss is paying for my time and I shouldn't abuse that by wasting time on witnessing conversations'. Again, this is not the whole truth. The whole truth includes several facts. First, who is your ultimate boss? Obviously the one who said, 'Go and make disciples.' Second, telling others about your faith need not involve long converstions that divert huge chunks of time: it may be just in a passing comment during ordinary, everyday conversation. Third, by bringing the Christian faith to work, you are operating in the best interests of your employer! The person who learns to follow Christ at work by hearing his words *and putting them into practice* will perform better. Your boss will find it difficult to argue with that. Fourth, and very important, remember that not all your time with your colleagues is paid for by your boss. There will be breaks during and after work where conversations will flow. We'll visit this issue again later.

> ### • CASE IN POINT •
>
> Rachel works in a bank. A single lady with huge commitments inside and outside of work, she has made a point of inviting colleagues to her home on a regular basis. No agendas, just good food.

● ● ● ● ● ● ● ● ● ● ● ● ● ● ●

MEMO 19
Subject : 'I'm in the minority'

You may be the only Christian in your office. Some have told me that they know of no other Christian in the whole company. While this may make things difficult, it is also an immense privilege: if you're in such a position you are being entrusted with bringing the message to your colleagues. If you do feel you would like more support, why not link up with a para-church organisation or local church for some encouragement and extra resources? However, the mere fact that you are on your own should not deter you from speaking up. And remember, you are not really alone: Jesus promises he will never leave you to cope without him.

MEMO 20
Subject : 'I could lose my job if I speak up'

This too is part of the wider issue of standing up for what you believe. While it is possible, though unusual, to lose a job through taking a stand, as a Christian you cannot lose your security. God is your provider and his promise is that 'your Heavenly Father knows what you need'. Part of your outward journey on the Emmaus road will include learning to trust your God.

● ● ● ● ● ● ● ● ● ● ● ● ● ● ●

Now that we've knocked a few boulders out of the way, maybe we should start laying down some of the road.

MEMO 21
Subject : Getting to grips with the questions

INTERACTIVE 4

Draw up a list of the common questions that you get asked or you yourself ask about faith. Commonly, questions such as 'Is there a God?' or 'What about all the religions/suffering in the world?' feature on most lists. See if you can come up with a top twenty.

● ● ● ● ● ● ● ● ● ● ● ● ● ●

MEMO 22
Subject : A three-way look at the questions

As you look at your list of questions (or think about it, if you didn't write it down), let me highlight a few of the issues you will need to bear in mind as you embark on the Emmaus project. On top of their religious concerns, everyone has questions about life. These will include issues such as 'How can I be happy?', 'How can I find meaning, love, peace of mind or purpose?', 'How can I cope with stress, sexuality, pressure or grief?', 'How can I be a competent husband, father, wife, mother, worker, son, daughter?' Keeping these common, human questions in your mind will help you remember that the Emmaus road approach is about encouraging people, not winning arguments.

Take a second look at your list. If it is typical, it will include questions about what you believe and questions about how you behave. In other words, there are Emmaus road questions and Damascus road questions. Some of them are much more to do with the experience of being a Christian than the theory of being a Christian. Here again, it is vital to remember File 1 and its advice about what it is really like to be a Christian.

As you look at your list for the third time, you may notice that it focuses on only a limited number of issues. This is true of everyone's list. There are not 2,000 questions which people raise about the Christian faith; there are usually only around twenty. This ought to be a great relief to you.

● ● ● ● ● ● ● ● ● ● ● ● ● ● ● ●

MEMO 23
Subject : Learning to give sensible answers

When a question about life arises with a colleague, you will need to think hard and quickly about how you answer. As you do so, you will need to make a swift assessment of why the other person is saying these things. Is this an important question to them or just a matter of vague interest? Is it a genuine question or a wind-up? Is the question being asked out of anger, hurt, ignorance or bad experiences of religion? If you don't know, you can always ask your colleague why he or she is asking the question.

Of course, the more you know your colleagues generally, the easier it will be to have meaningful conversations with them. Remember that having a discussion about God may be much easier for them than for you. You bring all kinds of anxieties about wanting to communicate your faith; they may simply be curious. Being aware of this should take the pressure out of the situation.

After your quick assessment, you'll need to have some sensible answers. Part of the challenge of the Christian life is to acquire, over the years, some short approaches and some longer ones to the list you have drawn up. Now there is no short cut here. Stacks of resources are available to you, to help you build up a repertoire of sensible answers. Books, videos, tapes and preachers abound. It's also an excellent idea to role-play some conversations with fellow Christians so as to sharpen up your responses. But it's vital that you become confident enough to rise to Peter's challenge to give reasons for your hope. One thing I can promise you: the more you prepare yourself, the more God will give you opportunities in your workplace. It's an encouraging spiritual fact that the more trustworthy you are, the more you will be trusted. So if you want the adventure of sharing your faith, work hard on the Emmaus road-building scheme.

It's outside the scope of this book to look into all the details of issues like why we trust the Bible, or the relationship between science and Christianity. However, I can suggest a few general principles for you to follow.

First and perhaps most vital of all, remember that Jesus' entire explanation to the disciples on the Emmaus road was 'concerning himself' (Luke 24:27). It's amazing how easy it is to forget that Christianity is about a person. Why do you believe in God? Because of Jesus Christ. Why do you take Genesis seriously? Because Jesus did. Why do you approach other religions the way you do? Because of Jesus Christ. Where do we find some answers in the face of suffering? In a crucified Jesus Christ. Why do you believe in life after death? Because of the risen Jesus Christ. No matter how long it takes, all evangelism and all witnessing are about enabling people to meet a person. These highways are for the Lord. When you've grasped this truth, your heart will 'burn within you' (v 32) and your confidence in your faith will overflow to your colleagues.

Second, when Jesus explained the truth to his disciples, he combined a gentle rebuke with a great deal of patience and courtesy. In the same way, when we encounter our colleagues, we may 'beg to differ' but always with courtesy and patience. Style matters as well as content.

Third, it's interesting to note how the two on the Emmaus road expressed their confusion. Even after Jesus had opened their minds, they didn't understand everything (v 31). It's vital that you have the ability to admit ignorance when you don't know the answer to a question. Your ignorance could take one of three forms. You may say, 'I don't know and I'm not sure anyone does.' It might be a case of 'I don't know but I will find out for you'. Or you may have to say, 'I don't know but I know someone who does', in which case you'll need to offer to set up a further meeting with that person. Whether you provide excellent answers or confessions of ignorance, you are still building the Emmaus road at work – and that's well worth doing.

• CASE IN POINT •

Paul worked as a senior manager in a financial institution. One weekend he received a phone call to tell him that one of his own staff, a young dealer, had been tragically killed in a car crash just half a mile from his home. The man was engaged to be married and had a four-month-old baby. On the Monday morning Paul visited the young man's family. After going to the funeral, he suggested to the family that it might be appropriate to hold a memorial service in the City. The family readily agreed and Paul, together with others, set about planning the event. Paul led the service and was also a speaker. Such was the impact of this young man's death on the City that the financial markets observed a one-minute silence, when foreign exchange dealers across the City stopped as a mark of respect.

For thirty-eight years Paul has been a friend to many of his colleagues in the City of London. Such was their respect for him that over two hundred of them turned up at his retirement event to wish him well, pay tribute to his life and work, and hear him explain one more time the meaning of the gospel.

MEMO 24
Subject : Commuting to Jericho – learning to love at work

It's ironic that a sarcastic self-justifying question elicits from Jesus Christ one of the most moving parables in the New Testament (Luke 10:25–37). The central figure, a Samaritan, was almost certainly on a business trip: Jesus describes him as a regular user of the road to Jericho. This being the case, he would have had every reason to be too busy to stop. The Samaritan would also have had little in common with the wounded traveller. The gap between them was not just a road's width: it was a cultural, religious and racial chasm. Jesus deliberately crafts the story to emphasise this point. The Samaritan businessman, however, engaged in several significant activities. He crossed the road, saw the man, took pity on him, treated him, took him to a better place and provided him with long-term support. This is the challenge of the Jericho road. It's about *showing love* in the workplace.

Love is not usually associated with the workplace unless it's in the context of office affairs. I would like to suggest, however, that it is vital to explore what it means to express love and compassion at work. This is particularly difficult when all the received wisdom declares that relationships at work must be formal and professional. I hope I will be able to show you that professionalism and real Christian love are not incompatible. As we do this together, we will construct our third road – the one to Jericho.

● ● ● ● ● ● ● ● ● ● ● ● ● ● ●

MEMO 25
Subject : Crossing the road

The behaviour that first distinguished the Samaritan from the other two travellers, both of whom were religious, was that he crossed the road to the wounded man. This simple act – summarised by Jesus in the words 'came to where he was' and 'he went to him' – represents a profound behavioural challenge for Christians at work. On a recent training course a questioner asked how he could take his witness further with his colleagues. 'I've explained the gospel to them,' he said. 'I work well at my job. But they just don't seem to be interested in my faith or in coming to church.' Without putting down any of what this man was doing, which seemed to me to be totally honourable, I gently enquired as to whether he ever socialised with his colleagues at work, either through work 'dos' or during lunch breaks. His answer was no.

I might have asked, 'Do you ever go to where they are?' Unfortunately, this working man was attempting to communicate his faith outside of the context of quality relationships. For many, the first meaning of crossing the road will be simply to spend time with colleagues on a more regular basis, with nothing on the agenda but friendship. This may involve going out at lunchtimes or after work, to Christmas parties or leaving 'dos'. It may involve a game of golf or ten-pin bowling, or a visit to a show. At its simplest, it just means spending time with people. The Samaritan just went over to where the man was.

● ● ● ● ● ● ● ● ● ● ● ● ● ● ● ●

MEMO 26
Subject : Relationships are messy

The wounded traveller was not a pretty sight. Blood and filth covered his battered and bruised body.

Now I'm not suggesting that you cross the road as a perfectly well-rounded individual to help your poor, dysfunctional colleagues. They may even appear to be more together than you. Whatever their state, however, you will encounter messiness. You may find the humour filthy and the language offensive. You may discover messed-up lives or unhealthy attitudes. But you will also discover real kindness and human dignity, coupled with loyalty and openness. In short, a real messy picture. Messiness is a hallmark of life on all the roads, but particularly the Jericho road of love. Remember that as the Samaritan crossed the road he didn't suddenly lose his race, gender, history or beliefs; he just went as he was to the wounded man where he was.

INTERACTIVE 5

If you are in a group, you might like to use these questions as 'points to ponder' or discussion starters.

What are the main opportunities in the working week to meet with others?

What are the main opportunities in the working year to meet?

What sort of opportunities could be created that currently don't exist?

What would it take to invite my work colleagues to my home?

How do I currently feel about my relationships at work?

● ● ● ● ● ● ● ● ● ● ● ● ● ● ●

We hear a lot about 'people skills' in the workplace today. Managers get sent away or consultants are brought in to impart these vital characteristics. Although there is an element of technique in both acquiring and using these skills, they are more than mere techniques. Some, on reading the next three memos, will feel that the skills described already come quite naturally to them. That's OK; you're that type of person. But others will discover some useful tools. All, I hope, will recognise the need for growth. Doing the work of developing these skills, whatever your current level of ability, is a labour of love. It's part of the cost of the Jericho project. Your willingness to pay that cost is an indication of the respect you have for your colleagues and your desire to serve the Lord at work.

So what are these skills? I'll group them under three headings, keeping the links with the Samaritan's behaviour.

MEMO 27
Subject : Connecting with people

You're at an office 'do' or out to lunch with some colleagues. How might things progress?

The Samaritan allowed himself to get involved. He didn't just look; he took in what he saw. He allowed what he saw to get to him. In your case, it may be that the needs of an individual are really not that obvious. The way you are likely to discover other people is through open questions.

It has been my experience that very few people have good conversational skills. The first step, I would suggest, is learning to ask good questions. If you've ever had the experience of meeting someone for the first time and swapping a little bit of biographical information, only to discover that you are rapidly running out of things to say, you'll know about the need for this skill.

Good conversational questions must be open questions. Open questions are ones which cannot be answered 'Yes' or 'No'. They often start with the words 'How?' or 'Why?' or 'What do you think?' Learning to ask them is nowhere near as simple as it sounds and requires a great deal of creativity on the part of the questioner. Earlier on, we used the image of crossing the road to describe the process of coming to where people are. There is another aspect to this. In order to ask good questions, you will need to acquaint yourself with the culture of today. This is not a chore: it is immensely rewarding and will involve reading what some of your colleagues read, listening to what they listen to, finding out what interests them. Chances are, of course, that many of these will already overlap with your own interests. In doing this pleasurable activity, you will not only increase your ability to ask good questions and engage in intelligent conversation, you will also communicate that you as a Christian live in the same world as everyone else.

Of course, I'm not suggesting you become an expert on every topic under the sun. In fact there will be times when you encounter something about which you know absolutely nothing. Here, in all humility, you can express a willingness to learn: 'Tell me more about Icelandic nose harps. I know nothing about the subject'. This type of approach will lead you to discover a vital truth: everybody has something that matters to them. If you ask, eventually you'll discover hobbies, beliefs, ideas, opinions or experiences which will open your eyes to the person in front of you.

Jesus went out of his way to connect with individuals. He told stories about individuals. He raised three individuals from the dead – an *only* son, an *only* brother and an *only* daughter. People warmed to him because individuals mattered to him. If you take an interest in the lives of your colleagues, they will almost always warm to you.

Asking questions is not the only aspect of this. It may be that you need to look fairly carefully at someone's mannerisms or tastes in order to engage with their world. Absenteeism or failing to meet deadlines may be signs of stress, signs that a caring person should try to read. It's particularly important to be sensitive to colleagues in what could be described as 'displacement moments'. These are times when change is high on the agenda and people feel displaced from their normal routine or environment. So when someone new arrives in your company or department, when someone is moved upwards or sideways, when someone is about to leave, they will be particularly open to a caring approach. The source of this feeling of displacement may, of course, be outside the workplace – a child starting secondary school or a partner leaving home. Being sensitive is not spectacular; it's a quieter approach that takes us on to our next 'people skill'.

• CASE IN POINT •

Paul and Kim are partners in an advertising and promotions company. Mid-morning, on a not untypical day, Paul received a knock on his door from one of the managers. One of the sales team had just received a phone call bearing the totally unexpected news that his father had died. Apparently the salesman, John, had not spoken to his father for many years. He was so shocked by the news that his perplexed manager could think of nothing else but to bring him to Paul's office. Paul brought in Kim, took over from the manager, and together they listened to John's story.

During a conversation that lasted no more that fifteen minutes, Paul and Kim tried carefully to talk of God's love and eventually asked John if they could pray for him. John agreed, although he had never really prayed in his life before this moment. Paul was seated behind his desk and Kim was standing at the back of the office, both of them four feet or so away from John. As they were, they closed their eyes while Paul and Kim prayed very simple prayers concerning the peace of God, comfort for John's mother and an awareness of the presence of God in this difficult situation.

When they had finished praying, John sat still with his eyes closed for a further two minutes. Under normal circumstances two minutes passes very quickly, but in this situation it felt like a long time. When he eventually opened his eyes he thanked the others, saying that he really felt loved.

'Thank you also for putting your arm round me,' he said 'I really appreciated that.'

'We didn't,' said Paul.

John insisted that someone had put an arm round

him while they were praying. Kim and Paul assured him that neither of them had moved from where they were, behind the desk and the back of the office, nor had one of them put a hand on his shoulder. Finally, they arranged for someone to drive John home.

John was so moved by the whole experience, he started to ask questions. After attending a 'just looking' group at a local church, he became a Christian.

● ● ● ● ● ● ● ● ● ● ● ● ● ● ● ●

MEMO 28
Subject: Listening to people

In the course of my work I have met thousands of people, but I can count on the fingers of two hands those I have met who really knew how to listen. It may be that I am so unspeakably boring that no one can be bothered to listen to me, but I prefer other explanations!

Listening is a dying art, yet listening is like bandaging wounds and pouring on oil and wine. It is one of the greatest compliments you can pay to anyone. I would suggest to you that listening is one of the highest expressions you and I can give of divine love. Our God is a God who listens, and it is in listening that we introduce people to his love. James, the brother of Jesus, tells us to be quick to listen and slow to speak (James 1:19). He spoke out of experience, since he had almost certainly worked with Jesus in the carpentry business and had taken quite a while to come round to being a disciple of his older brother and colleague. So maybe he was too quick to speak and too slow to listen, and was writing these words with a tinge of regret.

Listening is an all-embracing activity, not just the gap between the two things you want to say. This all-embracing activity involves a physical attitude which includes the use of the eyes, the arms and the way we sit or stand. The way people communicate that they are listening will vary from culture to culture. My wife is Portuguese. If you want to communicate that you're listening in her family, you have to talk at the same time.

Love will learn to communicate that it is listening. Listening requires an inner attitude of patience, hearing between the words to catch their meanings, hearing unspoken words, and sometimes shutting up your own reactions so that you can hear what is actually being said. The Bible is full of exhortations to listen: 'Does not the ear test words as the palate tastes food?' (Job 12:11); 'Hear, my child, and be wise' (Prov 23:19); Solomon himself prayed for a heart with the skill to listen (1 Kings 3:5–9). After you've asked your questions, listen hard to the answers. In so doing you will give your colleagues a great gift, and it's an excellent working practice.

● ● ● ● ● ● ● ● ● ● ● ● ●

MEMO 29
Subject: Responding to people

Having asked, having listened, there comes a time when you must respond; you must give yourself away. The Samaritan made an accurate assessment of the situation and provided an appropriate response. He did not campaign for safer conditions on the Jericho road or attempt to discuss the history of the relationship between the Jews and the Samaritans with his wounded fellow traveller; rather, he responded to him.

You may need to open up to your colleagues about your

own experiences and perhaps explain how your faith relates to them (like the music industry executive who was able to help a grieving colleague through his experience of his own mother's death from cancer). It may mean expressing an opinion in a way that contributes to a debate, or merely saying something Christian on a relevant topic. Whatever it means, there are a few things to bear in mind when you respond to people.

First, don't take yourself too seriously. People already have an image of Christians as dour, negative, humourless killjoys. The irony is that the more seriously you take yourself, the less seriously others will take you. The best reference for a job that I ever had was from an atheist senior colleague who wrote to the Christian organisation to which I applied: 'This man should not have this job. His sociable nature and humorous character will do much damage to the cause of atheism.' I didn't get the job but I was delighted with the reference. He had realised that I would die for some causes but was quite prepared to laugh at the trappings of my religion.

Second, it's OK to be emotional. The Samaritan felt very strongly about the wounded traveller – Jesus describes him as having pity on him. Jesus himself wept, got angry and passionate. British culture is not naturally expressive, but Christianity is more than just cultural. So include your feelings as you open up to others.

Third, as you ask and listen, opportunities will come your way to express your beliefs and your compassion verbally or in other ways. Seize them. And when you do seize them and say something, avoid Christian jargon like the plague. Use ordinary language.

It may be that you need to pray with a colleague or help them with a difficult project. Make whatever you do fit the need of the person for whom you are doing it. In so doing you are taking people into your world where they can meet Christ.

The Samaritan put the traveller on his own donkey, took him to his regular inn (judging by the innkeeper's trust in his credit line). In short, he took him to a better place. As you build the Jericho road of love in your workplace, you may or may not become more popular. But you certainly will take people to a better place.

INTERACTIVE 6

It may be helpful to use this interaction as a quick self-assessment.

Write down the names of three of your colleagues and then what you know about:

> Their hobbies;
> The names of their partners;
> What really matters to them;
> What struggle they are currently experiencing.

INTERACTIVE 7

Here's an exercise to help you focus your mind and practise listening. You'll need to do it with a group. Take two minutes to do each step:

1 Divide into pairs with someone you don't know especially well.

2 Find out as much as you can about your partner.

3 Let your partner find out as much as he or she can about you.

4 Explain sin to your partner, using no Christian jargon.

5 Let your partner explain to you how to become a

Christian, using no jargon.

6 Explain why being good enough is not good enough.

7 Let your partner explain the meaning of the cross to you.

8 Debrief together on how difficult or easy this exercise was for you.

After you have debriefed, answer the question at the end of the chapter.

• CASE IN POINT •

Isabel runs the media resources department in an inner-city secondary school. Because it is on the top floor of the older part of the building, there is an element of self-containment about the department. This does not make it isolated, however. Staff members constantly visit the department to enlist its services.

Isabel has made a point of creating an environment of peace in the offices. The walls are decorated with colourful and relaxing samples produced by the department. The rooms are tidy, even during frantic and busy times, and pleasant music plays in the background. Staff members regularly comment on the oasis of peace when they visit. The peace has nothing to do with the absence of work, since the department is constantly under pressure to meet deadlines and deliver results. It has to do with Isabel's approach.

A common task performed by visiting staff members is to photocopy documents for educational purposes. Sometimes there are queues and sometimes there is just one person waiting while the machine does its work. It's at these times when Isabel will often enquire as to how a staff member is doing. By her friendly and sensitive questioning, many a stressed staff member has taken the opportunity to de-stress for a while. Occasionally, Isabel has prayed with a colleague, and at other times she has made helpful suggestions concerning the professional or personal struggles they are facing. One colleague was struggling with a difficult toddler; another with the aftermath of a break-in at her flat; another with some management issue. People generally leave the department feeling better than when they arrived. It's not in Isabel's job description as such, but the impact on school morale is real enough.

INTERACTIVE 7 CONTINUED

Did you use any of the information learnt in steps 2 and 3 to help you explain the Christian concepts in steps 4–7 in a relevant manner to your partner? For example, I was once explaining the meaning of the cross to a telephone engineer. I asked him what was the meaning of a connection charge. When he told me, I explained to him that this too was the meaning of the cross. If you listen hard enough, a person will tell you how to communicate the gospel to them in ways which make sense to them. They will give you insight into their world and they will give you concepts you can use as vehicles of communication.

Executive summary for the busy and lazy

Our task is to build a Damascus road where lives are changed, an Emmaus road where faith is explained, and a Jericho road where love is expressed; friendship and faith at work involve changed working practices; working practices involve use of time, words, money, conflict as well as learning to enjoy work; witness involves learning to explain faith in today's culture and dealing with our own hesitations as well as the questions of other; there is only a limited number of questions people ask; friendship at work includes expressions of love; good conversations express loving attitudes; conversations require learning to ask, listen and speak; love at work means getting involved with others; people become Christians because they become convinced that it works, that it's true and that love is available, even in the workplace.

CLOSURE

Our voicemail system is being repaired.
This is a person speaking.

Norman Weed

MEMO 30
Subject: Crossroads, bridges and rivers

At the beginning of this book I invited you to build a bridge
from your current level of competence, which would connect with the liberating truth that witnessing at work is all
about being yourself at work. I hope by now that you will
not only have built this bridge but are beginning to let the
truth set you free. It seems to me that three-quarters of the
task facing us humans is to get in touch with our humanity.
Witnessing has become such a theological and religious
affair, it has been consigned to the church's mission programme. Surely one of the major lessons of the incarnation
is that when God wanted to communicate with us he became
human. It is as if God took off his glorious clothes and put

on his working suit; he put on the human body and in it learned to do the work of a carpenter.

Trying to work out how to represent him where we work is a struggle, yet our witness lies in that very stuggle. It is as we wrestle with the real issues that people can see our successes and failures in the context of a Christian life. The difference between our humanity and his is that he never sinned; but the power of our witness is that, in spite of our sin, there is a route to forgiveness, peace of mind and best practice. We've been woken up to the work of God.

Our building, however, must not be confined to bridges. If you have been reading between the lines, you will have noticed that the three roads we described related to the things which Paul argues will last forever. The Damascus road is all about faith; the Emmaus road is about hope; and the Jericho road is about love. These three will remain (1 Cor 13:13). The building projects I've described are a huge challenge but they are also a great adventure. Damascus faith will stretch you to the limits; Emmaus hope will give you divine heartburn; and Jericho love will drive out your fear. This is not the time to shrink, be fainthearted or fearful. God, the Master Builder, is at work, and invites you and me to join in the task of building. As I have researched this book and as I speak on workplace issues, story after story have come my way which inspire me to believe that the workplace is possibly the place where God is most active. This is not unrelated to the fact that the workplace is the place where humans are the most active.

So I encourage you to build your bridges so that you can cross the rivers of doubt. I urge you to build your roads so that your colleagues can meet your Lord. It is hard work but it is surely worth it. Work well.

● ● ● ● ● ● ● ● ● ● ● ● ● ● ●

MEMO 31
Subject : 'Yes, but...'

There is always a possibility in a book like this one of laying down some principles only to find someone saying, 'Yes, but you don't understand my place of work.' Today's workplaces vary greatly in their style and approach. I freely admit that some working cultures make human contact almost impossible. The time pressure coupled with the working environment drive people apart rather than together and conversations are restricted to instructions rather than interactions. I would maintain that even in such environments we should attempt to put the principles of friendship evangelism into practice while recognising the severe limitations placed upon us. It may even be that the primary focus of your witness will have to be outside of the workplace, in which case you'll need to wake up to something else and read other books. Even so, you will not be able to bypass the need for friendship.

There is a second 'Yes, but...' which I want to acknowledge. Some personalities are simply more friendly than others – we are made in a variety of configurations. If you are naturally shy and reserved, you may find friendship evangelism extra hard. I would like to say two words of encouragement to you. First, no one who meets me believes me when I tell them that I'm shy. The truth of the matter is that naturally I'm a classic introvert. God has taught me how to open up and, as I have wrestled with these principles, I have learnt to share my faith. Second, friendship is not just for the extroverts. Shy people need friends as well. My suggestion is that you do not try to be what you are not but become who you are in Christ. This will inform your working practices, your ability to explain and your capacity to love.

My last 'Yes, but...' concerns your relationship with your

church. It seems to me that the key to improving the link between Sunday and Monday is *friendship*; to be specific, friendship with your pastor or vicar. He or she is a person at work who needs your support in order to do their job, and their job is to help you to do yours. I've lost count of how many times I've heard one person say of another, 'He or she does not live in the real world.' The truth is we *all* live in different realities. It is my hope that we can all help each other 'wake up to work'.

RESOURCES

THE WORKNET PARTNERSHIP

The WorkNet Partnership was founded by Geoff Shattock in January 1997 in order to connect, equip and resource Christians in the workplace so that they can integrate their faith with their work and communicate it healthily to others.

CHURCH-BASED TRAINING

If you are concerned about the church end of things, the WorkNet Partnership has a day of training and conference specifically designed for churches. Called 'Wake Up to Work', it covers areas such as calling, witnessing at work, balancing home with work, and helping clergy and laity to understand each other's perspective on work. (It is vital that clergy be seen as a group of people 'at work', and that their pressures and challenges are recognised alongside those of the laity).

METASKILLS ®

At the work end of things, The WorkNet Partnership has a range of stress management and other training which is ideal for human resources, training or personnel departments. As a physiologist and theologian, the national director has specialised in stress management training from a Christian perspective. It is strategic to take such training into companies or school INSET days to reduce stress levels as well as to introduce Christian values. http://www.metaskills.org.uk

OTHER WORKNET RESOURCES

Workaholics Anonymous is a small-group approach to the issue of faith and work. One such is running in a pub in Mayfair, where a group of Christians in senior (or executive) positions meet to support and understand one another in the workplace. Many churches find that their relationship with the Partnership starts with a Sunday service on taking faith to work. For individuals, the partnership scheme provides a way of networking with like-minded Christians

'Wake up to Work' – *the album*
This is a multi-purpose recording containing thought-provoking commentaries on workplace issues. First broadcast on Premier Radio, the pieces have brought encouragement to thousands in their places of work. Discover, with Levi and Zacchaeus, the essence of calling at work. Understand the impact of words on colleagues. See team work in a new light. Receive advice on when to stop, along with help under pressure or with stress, fear, competing priorities, awkward bosses and moral dilemmas. *Wake up to Work* (volume one) may be used by individual Christians for personal inspiration or by groups as discussion starters.

Wake up to Work is available priced £9.50 (CD) and £7.50 (cassette). Order on tel 0171 649 9643 or from the Church Pastoral Aid Society, CPAS catalogue number 00050 (CD) or 00084 (cassette).

If you want help with faith and work issues, contact The WorkNet Partnership, 56 Baldry Gardens, London SW16

3DJ; tel 0181 764 8080, fax 0181 764 3030. E-mail: train-ing@worknetpartnership.org.uk or visit the website at http://www.worknetpartnership.org.uk

● ● ● ● ● ● ● ● ● ● ● ● ● ● ●

FURTHER RESOURCES

The Centre for Marketplace Theology operates in the City of London to encourage and build up Christians who work there. Contact David Prior at 13 Pensioners Court, The Charterhouse, London EC1M 6AU; tel 0171 336 7204. E-mail: dprior.cmt@city.co.uk

The International Christian Chamber of Commerce seeks to resource those in the business world. Contact ICCC at 51 Peverels Wood Avenue, Chandlers Ford, Eastleigh SO5 2BS; tel 01703 251588. E-mail: international.office@iccc.se

● ● ● ● ● ● ● ● ● ● ● ● ● ● ●

PUBLICATIONS

Thank God It's Monday by Mark Greene, published by Scripture Union.

Work Well, Live Well by David Westcott, published by Marshall Pickering.

ETHOS magazine (every two months), tel 0870 902 5400.

God@Work video: 'A vision for workplace ministry' consist-ing of two 20-minute films focusing on God's view of work.

God@Work audio tapes feature seven talks on workplace issues. Video £12.50 and tapes £19.95 (plus £1.50 p&p), Available from LBC Media, London Bible College, Green Lane, Northwood HA6 2UW; tel 01923 826061.

Other titles in the 'Relating Good News' series include: *Friendship Matters*, by David Spriggs and Darrell Jackson; *Sharing the Salt: Making Friends with Sikhs, Muslims and Hindus*, by Ida Glaser and Shaylesh Raja; and *Man to Man: Friendship and Faith*, by Steven Croft.

The Scruples website, managed by YWAM Canada, lists 500+ marketplace ministries at http://www.scruples.org